EARLY K
OF ENGLAND

Written by J. M. Sertori
Illustrated by Jim Eldridge

CONTENTS

Collins

THE ROMANS LEAVE

Britain was part of the Roman Empire for nearly 400 years, but by 410 CE the empire was falling apart. Many parts were under attack from wild tribes, and the emperor called his armies back to defend Rome. The people of Britain were no longer considered part of the empire, and had no Roman troops to fight off raiders. There were a lot fewer people than there are now, so a small gang of armed men could be enough to destroy an unprotected village.

Hardly anyone was able to write, so the only way of preserving information was for parents to tell their children. Sometimes the facts got confused. Today, we often have to guess the truth by looking at **archaeology**.

HENGIST AND HORSA

In the 5th century, members of tribes called the Angles and Saxons sailed from Denmark to Britain, looking for new homes and farmland.

Newcomers weren't always unwelcome. Sometimes local people accepted them, or even married them and had families.

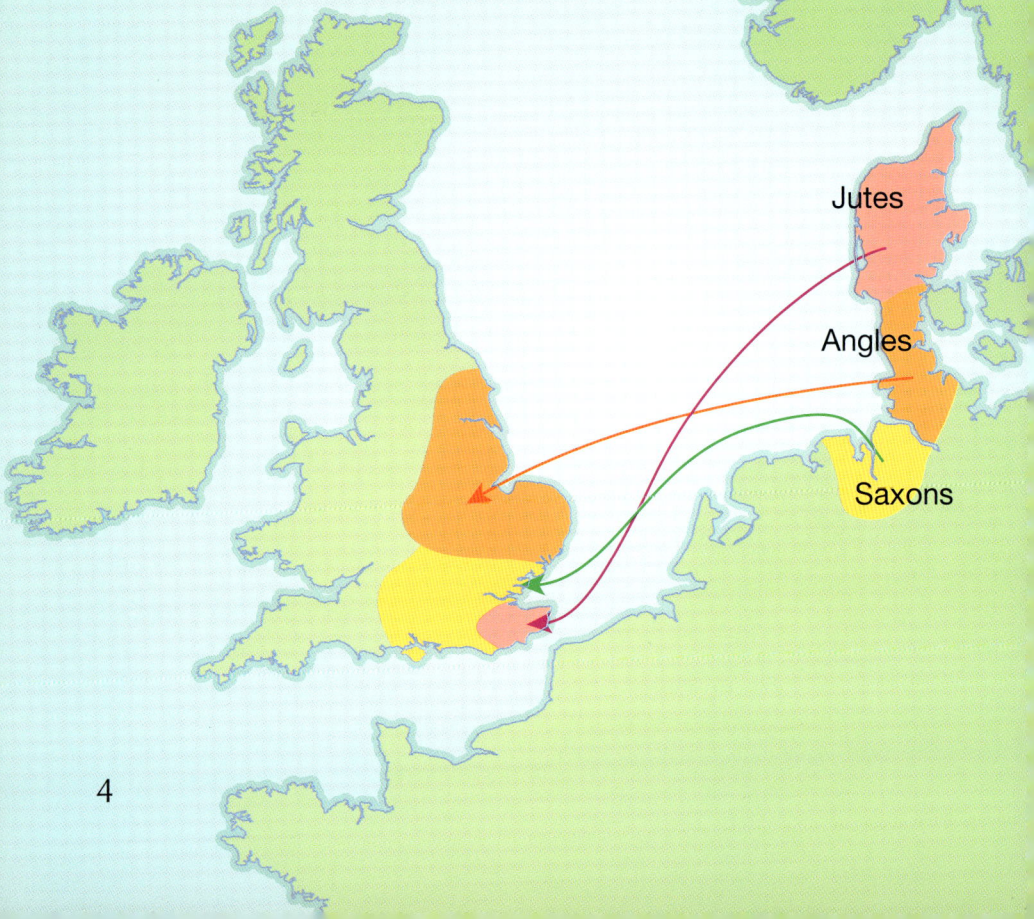

Jutes

Angles

Saxons

There are legends that say that some of these **settlers** were welcomed by Vortigern, a British **warlord** who hoped to use them in battles against his local enemies. He allowed the leaders Hengist and Horsa to settle in what's now called Kent, and he married Hengist's daughter, Rowena. Vortigern is remembered as the man who let the newcomers in. That was to lead to all sorts of trouble.

THE RUIN OF BRITAIN

In the beginning, the Angles and Saxons may have been paid to guard the coast against other invaders. But before long, they attacked their neighbours instead, and pushed the British far into the west of England.

SONGS AND STORIES

As people didn't write things down, they memorised poems and stories and told them to each other around the fire. These became legends.

There are many legends about a brave leader called Arthur, who fought the Saxons in 12 battles and finally halted them somewhere called Badon Hill. Many of the stories about him come from Wales, where a lot of the Britons settled. Although he is perhaps the most famous British king, he may never have existed, or could have been based on several real leaders.

SUTTON HOO

The Angles and Saxons were now known as the Anglo-Saxons, and had their own kings by the 6th century. Redwald was a powerful warlord of the East Angles. Old English books called him *bretwalda*, which means "Britain-ruler" or "wide-ruler". Redwald is likely to be the man buried at Sutton Hoo, a grave mound near Ipswich that tells us a lot about the period.

Lying beside the body was a helmet of iron with gold and gems. Its clothes had rotted away, but richly decorated clasps and brooches remained. Also in the grave were a shield with a Swedish pattern, and silver bowls from the Eastern Roman Empire. Being buried with precious items from far away meant you were a rich and powerful person.

The Sutton Hoo helmet was the most famous find in the grave. It had rusted over time and shattered when the roof fell in, turning it into a massive jigsaw puzzle to put back together.

THE KINGDOMS OF ANGLO-SAXON ENGLAND

Many of the place names we use today were first used in Anglo-Saxon times.

England was the land of the Angles, and included the North Folk (Norfolk), South Folk (Suffolk) and East Anglia.

The Saxons gave their name to Essex (from East Saxons), Wessex and Sussex (you can guess those two!).

Jutes from Denmark occupied an area they called Cent (Kent).

The centre of England was an Anglo-Saxon kingdom called Mercia, meaning "the border kingdom".

Northumbria used to be an Anglo-Saxon kingdom too. The name means "North of the river Humber".

In Wales, local rulers still called themselves "king of the Britons" for several centuries.

Celts

Anglo-Saxons

Edinburgh

Northumbria

Mercia

Wales

**East
Anglia**

Essex

London

Wessex

Winchester

Kent

Sussex

Hastings

Jutes

SERFS AND MASTERS

The local lord was seen as the owner of his lands, and the people who lived there were expected to help out in some way. Local people would have to help him bring in crops, repair roads, fight in his battles, or pay him taxes. If they refused, they could be thrown out of their homes and off their lands.

The Anglo-Saxon word for these people was "serfs", and they were often little better than slaves. Few of them stood much chance of getting away from their village and the job that their parents did.

THE ATTACK ON LINDISFARNE

Over the next 200 years, many Anglo-Saxons became Christians, like the Britons in the west, and people in many other countries in Europe. The Anglo-Saxon kingdoms became part of **Christendom** – the world of Christians.

They built churches and **monasteries**, and filled them with treasure, which they thought was safe because nobody would dare attack a "house of God".

They were wrong. In 793, raiders attacked the Holy Isle of Lindisfarne and burnt down the monastery. The raiders were Vikings – non-Christian warriors from Scandinavia. They carried out more and more raids until no town or church near a coast or river was safe.

JORVIK

Before long, an entire Viking army arrived in England, planning to stay for good. The king of East Anglia **bribed** them to leave by giving them horses, which they used to attack the northern kingdom of Northumbria. They killed the local ruler and turned what's now York into the Viking city of Jorvik. Vikings like Ivar the Boneless and Erik Bloodaxe would rule the region for the next century.

The Vikings in Jorvik settled down and became ordinary townsfolk.

bone and deer antler comb and case from Jorvik

There are no photos from Anglo-Saxon times, but this is what people think life was like in Jorvik.

ALFRED THE GREAT

For 14 years from 865, armies of Vikings from all over Scandinavia attacked England.

Alfred, the king of Wessex, organised the resistance against them. He seized 33 hilltops and strong points, many of which had been Roman forts. These *burhs* (forts) meant that his men were never more than a day away from repelling a Viking attack. He **fortified** bridges, to stop ships advancing upriver.

According to legend, he disguised himself as a musician and performed in the camp of the Viking leader Guthrum, to hear the Vikings' plans. Eventually, Alfred fought the Vikings to a standstill, and signed a **treaty** with Guthrum.

THE DANELAW

In the treaty between Alfred and Guthrum, the east of England was still controlled by the Vikings from Denmark – the Danes – and this area was called the Danelaw. It kept many Danish customs and laws.

The Anglo-Saxons were pushed west towards Wales as the Danes took over their farms and villages. The Vikings in the Danelaw had to defend themselves from other Vikings sailing across the North Sea to take their land.

Celts

Anglo-Saxons

Danes

Durham

York

The Danelaw

London

Winchester

THE ALFRED JEWEL

Alfred sometimes read for hours. He used a candle marked with lines showing how much time he had left. He may have been the owner of a richly decorated pointer, found in modern times, with the words "Alfred caused me to be made". It was used to hold the reader's place on the page.

THE CHILDREN OF ALFRED

King Alfred's children became rulers of Wessex and Mercia. Alfred's son, Edward the Elder, began his reign in 899 fighting his cousin, Athelwold, who tried to get support from the Danelaw. Edward won, reconquering much of the southern Danelaw.

Edward's sister Athelfled was a famous warrior and general, who'd fought off a Viking attack on the way to her own wedding. After the death of her husband, the king of Mercia, she called herself the Lady of the Mercians, becoming Edward's most powerful **ally**. Even the Vikings were afraid of her, and sometimes **surrendered** without a fight.

23

ATHELSTAN, THE FIRST KING OF ENGLAND

Edward seized Mercia after his sister's death, but he died six years later. His son, Athelstan, **inherited** both kingdoms, becoming the first true king of all of England.

Athelstan continued to attack the Viking kingdoms, ending in the Battle of Brunanburh in the north of England in 937. He led an army of Anglo-Saxons with Welsh allies, and fought against Vikings, Britons from Strathclyde, and Scots. He won, and England became a single country, from the Scottish border to the south coast.

MARKED FOR GREATNESS

When Athelstan was still a boy, Alfred gave him a red cloak, a jewel-studded belt and an expensive, decorated sword. Alfred may have been saying he thought Athelstan would make a better king than his father Edward.

WISE ST DUNSTAN

St Dunstan (909–988) was a **monk** from Wessex who became a powerful adviser to the early kings of England. Athelfled left him a lot of money, which he used to build monasteries and repair churches. His enemies accused him of witchcraft, and Athelred's son threatened to **exile** him, but changed his mind after he came to believe that Dunstan's powers had stopped his runaway horse from charging over a cliff.

Dunstan advised six kings during his 72-year life!

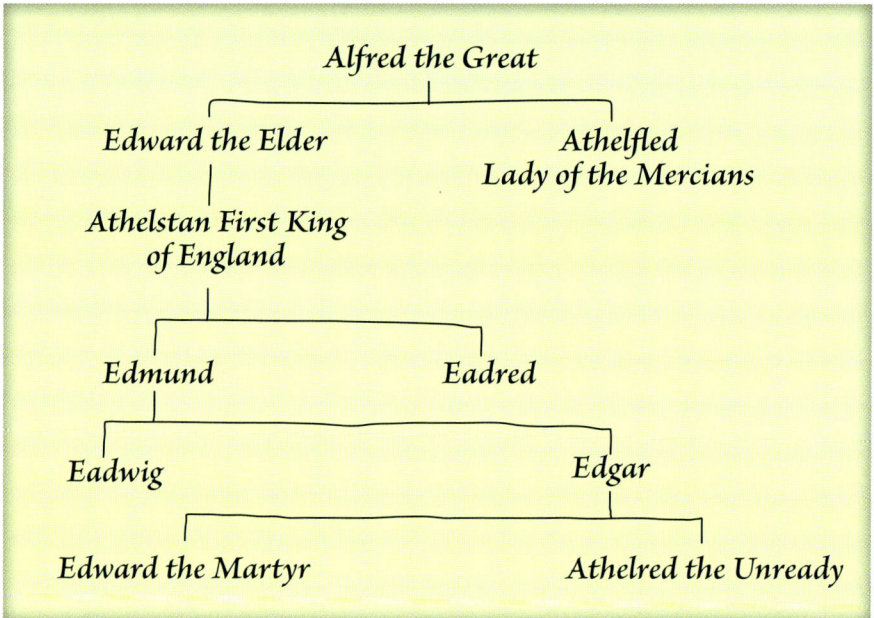

Alfred the Great

Edward the Elder

Athelfled
Lady of the Mercians

Athelstan First King
of England

Edmund

Eadred

Eadwig

Edgar

Edward the Martyr

Athelred the Unready

CLEVER MONKS

In Anglo-Saxon times, monks like Dunstan were almost the only people who could read. That meant they had a lot of knowledge. Sometimes kings listened to their advice, so some monks had a lot of power, too.

EDWARD THE MARTYR

After the death of Edgar the Peaceful in 974, his eldest son, Edward, became king when he was only 12 years old.

Edward was only king for three years, before he was killed as he climbed down from his horse at Corfe Castle in Dorset.

His half-brother Athelred's advisers had probably arranged the murder, and Athelred became the new king, bringing in a new group of supporters.

Athelred was also still a child and would lead his country into disaster. His nickname "the Unready" comes from *unraed*, meaning "badly advised".

In Anglo-Saxon times, kings and queens had total power over the people.
They could kill who they liked and then say it had been the right thing to do!

ATHELRED THE UNREADY

Athelred tried hard to keep his borders safe. After Vikings, led by Swein Forkbeard, raided London in 994, Athelred bribed them to stay away. Later on, such payments would be known as *danegeld* (Dane-gold).

But three years later, and each year after that, raiders attacked the coasts of England. Athelred suspected some of his people were helping them.

There were rumours that the Vikings had so much local support that they were planning another invasion, this time with support from the Danelaw.

ORDINARY PEOPLE

Most people were farmers and didn't take much notice of what rulers did. But it was hard not to notice if a battle happened near your village. Sometimes villagers were forced to fight in armies too.

St Brice's Day

When Athelred was told that Danes were plotting to kill him, he ordered the death of every Dane in the kingdom. On St Brice's Day, 13th November 1002, armed gangs of Anglo-Saxons began murdering every Danish man, woman and child they could find.

Peaceful Danes, who'd become ordinary farmers, locked themselves in a church. But the mob set fire to the building, killing everyone inside and destroying its contents as completely as any Viking attack would have done.

The St Brice's Day Massacre, as it was known, caused an unknown number of deaths in the Danish parts of England. One of the victims was Swein Forkbeard's sister, Gunhilde.

SWEIN FORKBEARD VERSUS EDMUND IRONSIDE

Even if Swein Forkbeard hadn't been planning another invasion before, he now had an excuse for one.
He invaded England three times, and fought many battles against Athelred's son, Edmund Ironside. Swein won in 1014, but died before he could be crowned king.

By 1016, England was ruled by Swein's son, Cnut, who married Athelred's widow, Emma, to help strengthen his claim to be king. Athelred's plans for keeping the Danes away had gone terribly wrong.

Bring your own gear

Anglo-Saxon soldiers usually had to provide their own weapons and armour, which was why only the rich got to be knights on horseback. Swords were expensive. The poorer men and serfs had to fight with spears and shields.

EMMA OF NORMANDY

Athelred the Unready married his second wife, Emma, when she was a teenager. Emma was the daughter of Duke Richard the Fearless of Normandy, a powerful man who'd been helping the Vikings by letting them dock their ships in his harbours. When Swein Forkbeard invaded, Emma fled to Normandy, but she came back later to marry Swein's son, Cnut. We know about Emma because she paid some monks to write her life story, although they only included the bits that made her sound beautiful and wise.

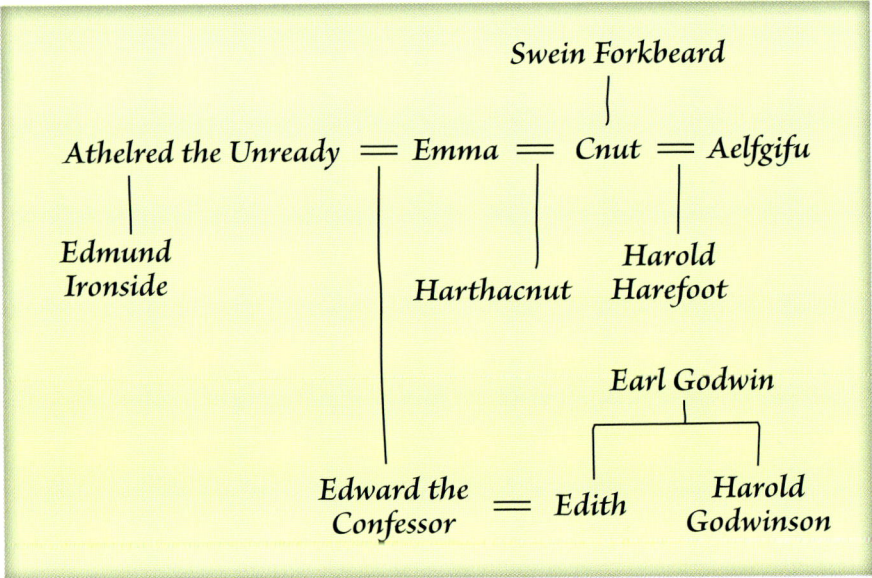

Swein Forkbeard
|

Athelred the Unready = Emma = Cnut = Aelfgifu
| | |
Edmund   Harold
Ironside   Harthacnut   Harefoot

Earl Godwin
|

Edward the = Edith   Harold
Confessor   Godwinson

ROYAL WOMEN

Women often had little power of their own in Anglo-Saxon times. But sometimes the mothers, wives and daughters were more clever than the kings themselves, so the kings often did as they were told.

Cnut the Great

Despite being one of the hated Danes, King Cnut is remembered as "the Great", partly because he supported the Christian church – it was monks who wrote the history, after all. But he was also the ruler of a large empire that included England, Norway, Denmark and parts of Sweden.

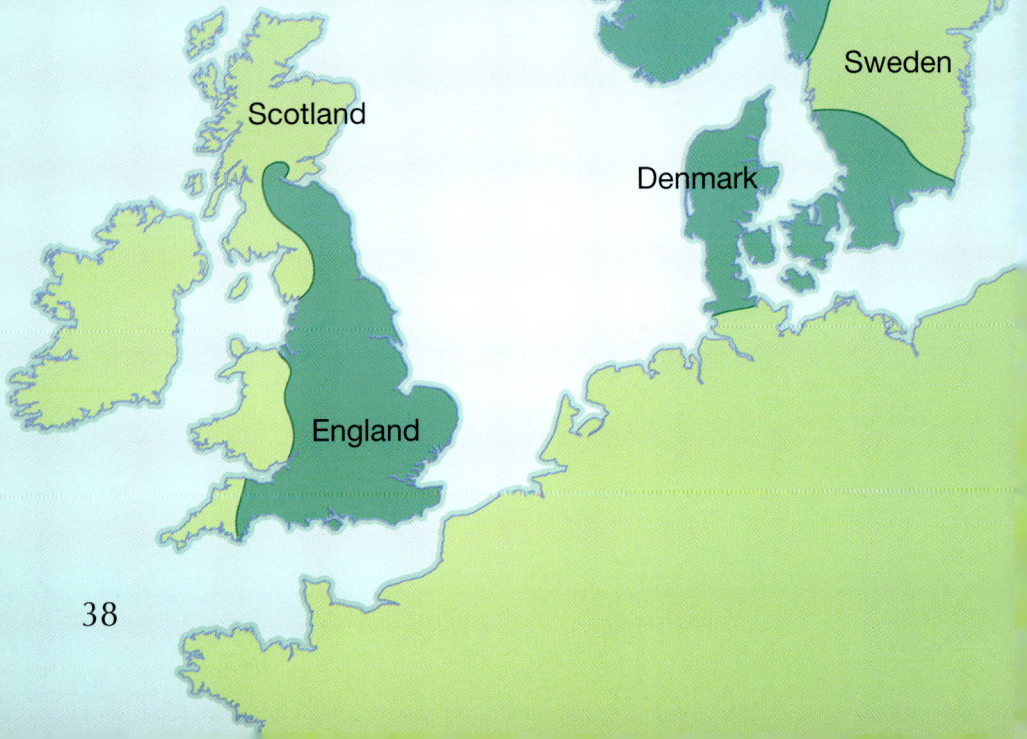

Cnut's empire

Norway

Sweden

Scotland

Denmark

England

The most famous legend of Cnut came from his refusal to listen to flattery from his men. When one boasted that Cnut could command the waves themselves, Cnut had his throne put on the beach, and demonstrated that the tide wouldn't turn at his command.

EDWARD THE CONFESSOR

Cnut's sons, Harold Harefoot and Harthacnut, each
ruled after him, but died of illness in the 1040s.
Legend amongst the English suggested that
they were "elf-shot", meaning cursed by magic.
Harthacnut's mother, Emma, seized the chance to put
his half-brother, Edward, son of Athelred the Unready,
on the throne instead.

Edward was called "the Confessor" because of his religious beliefs – he might have been happier being a monk. Since he had no children, it wasn't clear who should be king after him. But his Norman relative, William, claimed that Edward had promised the crown to him.

GRAND BUILDINGS

Most people still lived in simple wooden houses, but they built castles and other important buildings from stone.

41

THE BATTLE OF HASTINGS

Anglo-Saxon lords agreed that Harold, son of Earl Godwin of Wessex, would now be king. Soon after, Harold had to beat back a Norwegian invasion in the north of England. Although they won, his army then had to march south to deal with a second attack, by the Norman duke, William. William is said to have tripped on the beach as he landed, and then stood up claiming to have gripped the land in both hands.

Harold's exhausted men stood little chance. Harold was killed at the Battle of Hastings, and William became the first Norman king of England. He got the nickname William the Conqueror.

When William came to power, the Anglo-Saxon period ended. Since 1066, nobody has ever successfully invaded mainland Britain.

GLOSSARY

ally a person or group that gives help to another person or group

archaeology the study of ruins and buried objects to work out what happened in history

bribed paid someone to do something you wanted them to do – or to not do something you didn't want them to do

Christendom all the countries where people believed in Christianity

exile to send someone away and not allow them to return

fortified made a place or building strong so it could resist attack

inherited received something from someone who has died

monasteries places where monks live, and treasure is often kept

monk a Christian man who devotes himself to his religion and lives in a monastery

settlers people who move from one land to another and set up home there

surrendered gave up when you've been defeated in battle

treaty an agreement between rulers, usually to stop fighting or share land

warlord a ruler

INDEX

Early Kingdoms of Britain

Strathclyde

Northumbria

Norse settlements

Bath
possible site of the Saxon
defeat at Badon Hill

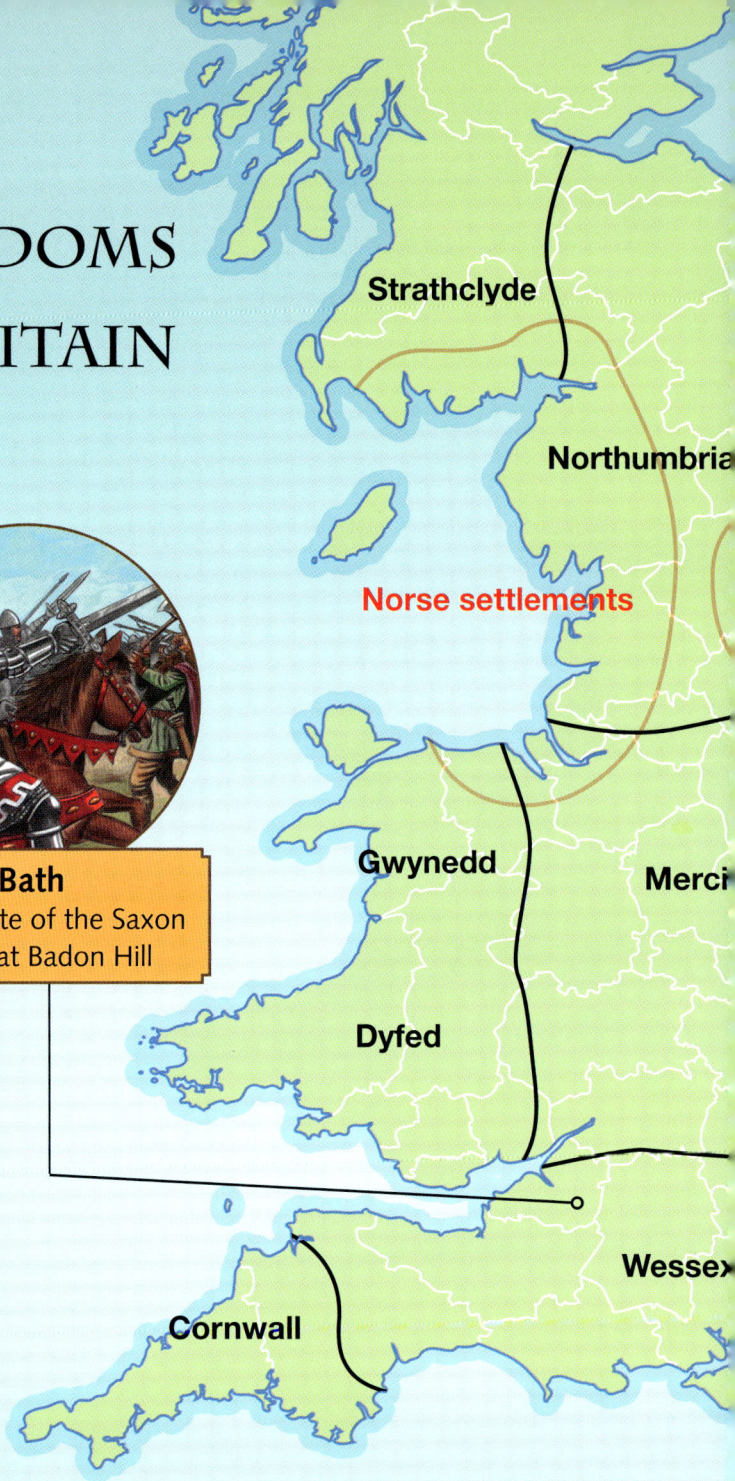

Gwynedd

Merci[a]

Dyfed

Wessex

Cornwall

Lindisfarne
site of earliest Viking attacks

York
formerly known as
Jorvik, a Viking town
in Northumbria

The Danelaw

Sutton Hoo
site of a grave mound where
Redwald may be buried

Hastings
site of William the Conqueror's
victory over Godwin's son, Harold

Ideas for reading

Written by Clare Dowdall, PhD
Lecturer and Primary Literacy Consultant

Reading objectives:
- retrieve and record information from non-fiction
- ask questions to improve understanding
- identify main ideas drawn from more than one paragraph and summarise ideas

Spoken language objectives:
- give well-structured descriptions, explanations and narratives for different purposes

Curriculum links: History – Anglo-Saxons, Scots and Vikings

Resources: mask making materials, paper and pens, ICT for research

Build a context for reading
- Ask children to imagine what it would have been like to be an early English king who followed the Romans' withdrawal in 410.
- Read the blurb and look at the front cover. Ask children to suggest what they think life might have been like for people living in towns and villages after the Romans left. Recall some of the things that the Romans introduced and achieved in England.
- Read through the contents together, practicing pronouncing the kings' names. Ask children if they are familiar with any of the names, and to share any knowledge.

Understand and apply reading strategies
- Read pp2–3 with children and support them to summarise the key information about the Romans' departure in concise bullet points.
- Ask children to read pp4–5 independently. Invite them to explain what they think a settler is, encouraging them to make connections to migration today. Check their ideas using the glossary.